Keys to Understanding Spiritual Understanding & Warfare

Keys to Understanding Spiritual Understanding & Warfare

Liberty Savard

Bridge-Logos *Publishers*

Gainesville, Florida 32614 USA

Spiritual Understanding & Warfare

Copyright © 2001 by Liberty Savard
Library of Congress Catalog Card Number: Pending
International Standard Book Number: 0-88270-847-3

Bridge-Logos *Publishers*

PO Box 141630
Gainesville, FL 32614
http://www.bridgelogos.com

DEDICATION

I dedicate this book to Guy Morrell, my publisher,
who has always been ready to help spread this message.

TABLE OF CONTENTS

INTRODUCTION

Most of the people in the world today have no idea whether or not any given Christian, Buddhist, Muslim, New Age seer, or Jehovah's Witness is making decisions and acting out of:

1. **their born-again human spirit linked with the Spirit of God,**

2. **the influence of demonic spirits, or**

3. **their own human souls.**

Do you automatically know the real source of another person's words and behaviors by becoming a

Christian? Not necessarily. Understanding the difference between souls and spirits cannot be learned from a daily Bible devotional reading or from a textbook in a Bible college. Nor does this **understanding** come from just praying. New Agers pray, satanists pray, Muslims pray, witches pray. There is nothing holy in the act of prayer in itself. God only involves himself in right prayers prayed by His people. More about **right prayer** later.

Spiritual understanding of another person's behaviors or words comes by consistently <u>practicing and acting upon</u> what you have read in the Bible, together with obedience to the Holy Spirit's responses to your prayers. This **understanding** belongs to those *" . . . whose senses and mental faculties are <u>trained by practice to discriminate and distinguish</u> between what is morally good and noble and what is evil and contrary either to divine or human law"* (Hebrews 5:14, *Amplified*).

How important is it to know where peoples' actions and behaviors originate? Watchman Nee says that "the greatest advantage in knowing the difference between spirit and soul is in perceiving the latent power of the soul and in understanding its falsification of the power of the Holy Spirit." That sounds pretty important.

Throughout the first section of Matthew 12, we see the Pharisees criticizing every move Jesus Christ and his disciples made. They inititally tried to cast doubt upon the miracles Jesus was performing by accusing Him of breaking the Jewish religious laws. Apparently having no religious law in question after Jesus healed the blind and mute, demon-possessed man, the Pharisees accused Him of healing by the power of Satan himself.

> *No longer able to point to Jewish law being broken, the Pharisees moved into trying to cause people to misunderstand the source of His words and actions.*

In Matthew 12:22 (*KJV*), we read that, *"Then was brought unto him one possessed with a devil, blind, and dumb: and <u>he healed him</u>, insomuch that the blind and dumb both spake and saw."* We are not told here that Jesus cast the evil spirit out of this person, we are told that Jesus HEALED this man. The original Greek word used here for healed is *therapeuo* (ther-ap-yoo'-o), which *Thayer's Greek-English Lexicon* #2323 says means: to serve, do service, to heal, cure, restore to health. This was not a demonic deliverance, yet deliverance ministries refer to this Scripture as a proof that Jesus was in the deliverance ministry the same way they are.

Matthew Henry says that Christ's "cure was very strange, because He healed him. <u>The conquering and dispossessing of Satan is the healing of souls.</u>"

Too often the Christian community has offered hurting believers three choices—none of which will bring healing and restoration to a wounded and needy mind, will, and emotions without a divine healing in the entire soul.

1. **The first choice is to simply accept that Jesus died to atone for our sins and to give us abundant life, and then start living like a whole person. Period. This is scripturally correct, but very hard to appropriate when your soul is in a full-scream panic about its pain, its unmet needs, and its sense of injustice.**

2. **The second choice is to get deliverance from demons. This is flawed for many reasons which will be covered later. Even if deliverance were a viable choice, if there was no cooperation of the soul to give up its wrong patterns of thinking and the strongholds it had erected to justify their existence— everything would revert back to the original demonic pattern in short order.**

3. **The third choice is to enter into extended Christian therapy which can include extensive digging around in the past.** *We cannot fix our present and embrace our futures by digging around in our pasts.*

Some Christian therapists really are standing in the gap for desperate people, holding on to their ragged souls until the clients get a breakthrough with Jesus Christ. Other Christian therapists, however, borrow liberally from the secular psychiatry/psychology industry. I read an interesting comment recently about Freud's strong influence on Christian counseling today, saying that he is one of a few men who continue to rule much of the world from their graves.

There is a better way to deal with our wounded souls and the interference of the forces of Satan. We are using secular methods to counsel our wounded, and we are fighting spiritual survival battles with Satan day and night. Meanwhile, the world is falling apart while people are dying of drugs and alcohol and AIDS, and children are killing each other at their schools. Yet we claim to have all authority and power, we shout at the devil, we draw "blood lines" on the floor to show Satan where he can and cannot cross.

What is wrong with this picture?

Authority, protection, and right standing in any area of life, natural or spiritual, can be severely hindered, <u>even rendered useless,</u> by the presence of open doors that an enemy can come and go through as he will. Leaders in the armed forces of the U.S. will tell you that <u>their highest levels of authority and power are useless</u> if there are open doors in their supply sources, communication lines, and battle planning rooms. There isn't a smart enemy alive who won't use those open doors to attack, slash, and burn—and the Christian's enemy is very smart. Don't ever be foolish enough to call him stupid, or to sing foolish songs about him. Jude 1:8-9 (*NIV*) states:

> *In the very same way, these dreamers pollute their own bodies, reject authority and slander celestial beings. But even the archangel Michael, when he was disputing with the devil about the body of Moses, did not dare to bring a slanderous accusation against him, but said, 'The Lord rebuke you!'*

We can close the doors of access in our souls and stop Satan's unimpeded harrassment of ourselves. You will find out how to do this in this book. Once we have begun to accomplish that, we need to begin to turn around the condition of our country, and the other countries of the world. We need to understand that for all the authority we say we have, we haven't really had much of a clue as to what to do with it. Then we need to begin to make some changes in how we are dealing with the destroyer.

Territorial spirits, principalities, and powers in high places find their access into or over geographical areas through the power released to them from wrong agreements of the souls of those in the area. It is a natural human desire to seek validation agreement with our negative feelings. This is especially true when the emotions are powerful and intense, such as grief, loss, anger, fear, bitterness, betrayal, unforgiveness, hatred, desire for revenge, etc.

In America, we have many displaced groups, races, and tribes who have been torn from their home lands or had their land torn from them by stronger and more aggressive groups or nations. Such corporate acts of man's inhumanity to man have created and continue creating massive wrong agreements in the minds, wills, and emotions of those who have been oppressed, plundered, enslaved, and wronged.

God's Word does not permit a sliding scale of whether or not we have a right to be angry and bitter at injustices to ourselves or others. He simply says that none of us are to let the sun go down on our anger (Ephesians 4:26). That is such a simple command, yet so very, very difficult for so many of us (if not all of us!).

In many areas revival has not come because of the darkness of the territorial spirits feeding off the corporate anger, fear, and pain of people in the area. Perhaps you are a part of a corporate group that is plagued with, even consumed by, anger, grief, pain, or fear. Perhaps you are one who simply wants all people to be free. Regardless of who we are, each one of us can be "doing" something in alignment with God's will that will help turn harsh, cruel consequences around wherever we are.

God has said in Isaiah 49:24-25 that captives <u>can</u> be taken back from the terrible one. To do so requires the unseating of the throne of the terrible one holding dominion over the land of the captives. We, the believers, are the ones who have the Keys of the Kingdom, given to us by Jesus Christ with all of His authority behind them. We are the ones of this day who are to dethrone the powers of darkness residing over our land. This will create an outpouring of grace for corporate right agreement in repentance and prayer, culminating in the healing of our land!

In 2 Chronicles 36 and Jeremiah 37, we read that the Israelites became more and more unfaithful to their God, taking up many of the ungodly practices of Babylon while in captivity. God continued to send messages as to how the Israelites could be free of their miserable lot, but they mocked His messengers, despised His words, and scoffed at His prophets while embracing the lies of their false prophets. God's prophet, Jeremiah, was very upset during this time at the number of <u>false prophets telling the captives that all was well, and Babylon would be broken instead of Judah.</u>

This is a frightening thought with so many today prophesying wealth and power and unlimited favor for the entire body of Christ. Such wealth and power and favor will not be poured out upon the Church unless there is a massive turning away from so many of our wicked ways.

After speaking vehemently to the Israelites about the false prophets, Jeremiah finally ceased trying to get the true Word of the Lord through to their darkened understanding. He wrote to the Israelites in exile and basically told them to just settle in for the duration of their captivity. In other words, <u>they had made their choice and now they would have to walk out to the</u>

bitter end the natural consequences of their earthly circumstances. We always have a choice. If we choose not to hear God's true Word, our self-wills may set our feet to walk out hard consequences to a bitter end.

Daniel seemed to understand there was another choice. He chastened himself and set his heart and mind to understand and pray, and a heavenly battle broke out to dethrone the ungodly "prince of Persia" controlling the principalities over the land. This prince was a territorial spirit who had been given dominion over Babylon because of the multiplied negative emotions and wrong agreements of the captives therein. This spirit smothered and blinded the Israelites' reasoning to the point of their ignoring God and rejecting His advances of grace. They perpetuated their own bondage, giving authority to the territorial spirit to hold dominion over them because of their corporate wrong agreements.

In Daniel 9:5-11 (*Amplified*), Daniel prayed and confessed the corporate wrong agreement of his people while in captivity:

> *We have sinned and dealt perversely and done wickedly and have rebelled, turning aside from your commandments and ordinances . . . . O Lord, righteousness belongs to you,*

*but to us confusion and shame of face
.... We have not obeyed the voice of
our Lord our God by walking in his
laws, which he set before us by his
servants the prophets.... Therefore
the curse has been poured out on us,
and the oath that is written in the law
of Moses the servant of God, because
we have sinned against Him.*

Then Daniel said (9:21-22, *Amplified*):

*While I was speaking and praying,
confessing my sin and the sin of my
people Israel, and presenting my
supplication before the Lord my God
... Gabriel ... being caused to fly
swiftly, came near to me ... and said,
O Daniel, I am now come forth to give
you skill and wisdom and
understanding.*

In Daniel 10:12-13 (*Amplified*), the angel of the Lord says to Daniel:

> *"Fear not, Daniel, for from the first day that you set your mind and heart to understand and to humble yourself (chasten yourself) before your God, your words were heard, and I have come in consequence of your words. But the prince of the kingdom of Persia withstood me for twenty-one days. But Michael, one of the chief of the celestial princes, came to help me. . ."*

As I travel across America, I have been in direct confrontation with territorial spirits on different occasions. The details of these confrontations are not important here, for the answers do not lie in focusing upon warfare with these demonic strongholds in a direct manner.

> *The answers lie in shattering the effects and influences of the multipled wrong agreements that are empowering these demonic princes to sit on their thrones.*

There are powerful demonic strongholds over Sacramento, CA where I live. I am never quite as aware of them as I am when I return from speaking engagements and step off the airplane in the Sacramento airport. From that moment on, through the next 24 to 36 hours, I frequently battle discouragement, depression, and darkness. The battle has become easier as I have been more aware of the sources of these negative feelings and addressed the evit spirits' tactics immediately.

God has told me to teach what must be dismantled and broken to unseat these spirits. He almost seems to be communicating what I remember saying to my squabbling children when they were were engaged in fighting with each other. Immediately they tried to detract me from my mission to stop the fighting by accusing each other of starting it. "He started it!" "She started it!"

I remember telling them, "I don't care who started it, I'm finishing it. I want this ended right now!" God seems to be saying that it doesn't matter who started it, He wants it ended.

God does not look down upon us and see any as having a favorite son or daughter status. He does not see us according to nationality, gender, wealth, education, race, or any other classification that man has come up with. He looks down and sees wounded, hurting, defensive, angry people jockeying for power and protection of their self-perceived rights. And one group's rights are always promoted at the expense of some other group's rights. He wants it ended.

I taught this message in one church that stands on the very ground of a former African slave holding pen in Alabama and felt the hatred of the territorial forces. It is not hard to imagine the corporate wrong agreements made there out of great fear, pain, grief, loss, anger, and hopelessness. I taught this message in a large city in Texas where something terrible had to have happened to cause great pain among the Hispanics, for I actually saw that territorial spirit manifest itself across the night sky. Corporate wrong agreements were made there out of great fear, pain, grief, loss, anger, and hopelessness.

I have taught this message in Canada, Washington, and upper Oregon and felt the incredible force of territorial forces over the Pacific Northwest. I have taught this message in Montana and seen breakthroughs in the territorial darkness.

Yet, all of the teaching, preaching, and breakthrough this message has brought has come without ever binding, rebuking, or screaming at any evil spirits. It has been accomplished through corporate prayer by all in attendance at meetings, prayers prayed out loud in one accord against the effects and influences of the wrong agreements of all of the people of the area. These corporate prayers were prayed as well for former agreements made years ago and then passed on from generation to generation.

I believe Daniel's prayers (that unseated the prince of Persia) are a valid pattern for future generations to use to unseat demonic princes over their cities! Daniel's 21 <u>days</u> of power prayers contained no declaration of authority, no commanding, no rebuking, nor casting down of satanic powers—all actions the unsurrendered soul loves to invoke. Daniel's power praying contained only humble confession, repentance, and pleas for mercy regarding the sinfulness of those who had spoken the wrong agreements.

> *If church bodies and intercessors' groups across our nation would consider just 21 <u>hours</u> of continuous corporate praying in right agreement after Daniel's fashion, what might happen?*

Many people groups have come into intensely wrong agreements (in God's eyes). Hurt and hate has been carefully passed from generation to generation, creating new wrong agreements. Massive corporate wrong agreements open the doors to demon-held dominions over geographical areas that <u>continue to perpetuate distrust, and hatred between people groups.</u>

Finding the answer to the divisions within our society began when many in the body of Christ, and many from outside of it as well, began to turn from their personal mindsets to seek reconciliation and forgiveness from those oppressed and downtrodden. This has driven out some of the wrong negative thought patterns and attitudes between the people of our nation. But victory will be the swiftest and the most powerful when the effects and influences of wrong agreements and walls between people begin to be torn down by those from within the very heart of the groups who have been hurt the most.

How can this happen? When all peoples agree upon one prayer, one plea, one common cry, one unified hope: *"Not my will, not my religious denomination's will, not my race's will, not my gender's will, not my culture's will, <u>but THY WILL BE DONE, O LORD.</u>"* There is not really any other direction we can ever move towards in true unity.

> ***Lord, you have said that if the people who are called by your name would humble <u>themselves</u>, pray, seek your face, and turn from their wicked ways, you would heal their***

land. We have sinned against you, Father. Forgive me and forgive the members of my family, church, culture, race, gender, and nation for our sins and wrong actions towards you and others.

Because of the oppression, pillaging, and abuse of those who have suffered in our land, there have been many wrong agreements struck in hurting, needy, angry, hating souls. Father, I loose, crush, and disrupt the controlling effects, influences, and power tactics of the territorial spirits that have moved into this area and are feeding off of those souls' pain, hatred, and fear. I loose the effects and influences of wrong agreements made by those now resident in the land. I loose the effects and influences still in place from the wrong agreements of <u>those who formerly lived</u> in this land.

I loose these territorial spirits' smothering clouds of hatred and fear that have caused the people of this the land to disengage from and distrust each other so much. I loose the generational bondage thinking patterns—

one hating, hurting, fearful generation teaching the next generation to hate, to hurt, and to fear. I loose, destroy, and shatter the effects, influences, and power of the multiplied wrong agreements that invading forces of darkness have moved in to feed off of.

I bind the minds, wills, and emotions of every person in this area to the mind of Christ. By abundant acts of your mercy and grace, open up avenues of pursuit for your people to earnestly search for right agreements in prayer with others. Show me what attitudes and fears reside within my own soul that have prevented me from doing this before now, and I will loose them.

Let your mighty Holy Spirit serve notice on the territorial spirits over this territory that there are people "doing" what needs to be done to unseat them. We will occupy the land and forever prevent their return. We will hold the territory as we all begin to agree that your will shall be done on earth, Father. Amen.

Please read the following questions and answers. It is my sincere hope that they will give you insight and encouragement to step beyond what you have understood about spiritual warfare. You have been involved in fights that were only designed by Satan to keep you busy. In fact it is Satan who has "taught" the current manner of spiritual warfare to the Church of today. There were no deliverance churches, or deliverance meetings in the New Testament Church.

It is time that you learned how to close the doors of your soul and become truly effective in disrupting the enemy's works on a much larger scale.

1

SPIRIT VERSUS SOUL

Question: *Why does Satan attack the soul? Isn't the spirit of a person what he wants?*

Liberty's Answer: Every person is a tripartite being—body, soul, and spirit. Satan's allowed realm of influence is in the soul because that is where the decisions of life are made (in the mind) and carried out (by the will). Once a person comes to Christ, his spirit is given new life and he (or she) becomes a child of God. The body and soul, however, are still in need of cleansing and renewal:

> ***Therefore, I urge you, brothers, in view of God's mercy, to offer your bodies as living sacrifices, holy and pleasing to God—this is your spiritual act of worship. Do not conform any longer to the pattern of this world, but be transformed by the renewing of your mind. Then you will be able to test and approve what God's will is— his good, pleasing and perfect will***
> (Romans 12:1-2, *NIV*).

Renewal of the mind brings it into alignment with God's Word and His will. A closed mind and strong will is going to resist the Word of God with all of its cunning and resources. Binding ourselves to the truth of God, to His will, and to the mind of Christ helps us to cooperate with this renewal by the Word of God. The Keys to the Kingdom are given to you so that you can work <u>with</u> this divine renewal process God wants to begin in you.

> ***And I will give unto thee the keys of the kingdom of heaven: and whatsoever thou shalt bind on earth***

> *shall be bound in heaven: and*
> *whatsoever thou shalt loose on earth*
> *shall be loosed in heaven*
> (Matthew 16:19, *KJV*).

Satan knows that if he can manipulate and control your soul through the fear tactics of his psychological warfare against your mind, he can influence your words and your behaviors. We have been given wonderful keys and weapons to bring our souls into alignment with the will of God and thereby block Satan's influences upon them:

> *The weapons we fight with are not the*
> *weapons of the world. On the*
> *contrary, they have divine power to*
> *demolish strongholds. We demolish*
> *arguments and every pretension that*
> *sets itself up against the knowledge of*
> *God, and we take captive every*
> *thought to make it obedient to Christ*
> (2 Corinthians 10:4-5, *NIV*).

Remember to bind your mind to the mind of Christ and your will to the will of God. Loose any thoughts that hinder you as a child of God with destiny potential!

3

Take captive every thought, releasing them to Christ, just as Paul declared in 2 Corinthians 10:5.

Question: *According to your knowledge, what is the difference between a demonic spirit and a stronghold? I've read your books, and you do not give a definite answer to this question. My question is: How does one know when they are dealing with a spirit rather than a stronghold in another person? I ask this because it came up in a conference that I attended. The guest speaker was casting out what she called spirits that to my understanding were strongholds. I need help understanding the difference.*

Liberty's Answer: A stronghold of the mind is **the arguments and reasoning that you use to defend your position or belief regarding something.** This easily translates into the logic, reasoning, rationalization, and justification you use to defend your right to make a choice you want to make. When this choice is in disobedience to God, the stronghold is your reasoning and excuses as to why you did it.

All of us have created strongholds to justify why we could not obey the Ephesians 4:26 command of God, for example, about dealing with our anger before the sun goes down. When we do that, verse 27 (*Amplified*) kicks in, *"Leave no such room or foothold for the devil—give no opportunity to him!"* Disobedience to verse 26 means you have just given the devil room, footholds, and opportunity in your life.

The enemy attacks through these open doors or opportunities that your soul creates by trying to justify ignoring God's will and pursuing your own. I've always had this mental picture of evil spirits driving past a Christian's house throwing pipe bombs, Molotov cocktails, and tear gas bombs in through open doors. The result is much destruction, loss, tears, and pain. The doors need to be closed to keep the enemy's harassment out.

When strongholds are destroyed and their doors of access are closed, I believe this cuts off the access of demonic interference in a Christian's life. However, there is great danger in Christians coming into agreement with spiritual leaders who tell them that they have an evil spirit in them, and then asking if they want to be rid of it. I have seen Christians (that I know do not have demons in them) respond to a spiritual leader calling them to come forward for prayer for demons. As soon as the people being prayed for agreed with the leader that they wanted to be free of an evil spirit in them, they began to show demonic manifestations.

Their wrong agreement allowed the spirits to harass their souls. Then their souls telegraphed the demon's harassment to their bodies, and the manifestations began happening. Be very, very careful about what you agree to in prayer with someone who believes they are moving in the realm of deliverance!

Question: *I've been a Christian for nearly ten years. Throughout that time, people have told me that God has a special plan for my life. I know other people who are newer in the faith than me, and it seems that they just instinctively know God's plan for them. I feel like I'm still sitting at square one, not moving anywhere. How can I know God's plan for me?*

Liberty's Answer: Your question is echoed by thousands of Christians around the world. The enemy delights in confusing believers in their efforts to understand how they were created to serve the Lord. This is a wrestling match I would like to help you get out of right now.

God loves you very much and He has a plan for your life. He wouldn't love you any more if you were moving at the speed of light in His destiny plans. And He wouldn't love you any less if you were completely failing to move in His plans at all. He simply loves you, and He has made you with a unique potential to bring joy and pleasure to Him in a way that no other person can.

> *There is no one on earth today who the same potential to fulfill the plans and purposes He has for you! So, you're not just a back up singer in the choir of your destiny—you are the lead singer!*

A major roadblock to knowing God's plan for you is your own understanding. Christians seem to <u>know</u> that God has a plan for them, they just don't <u>understand</u> how he is ever going to bring it to pass. I felt I was supposed to be preaching and teaching for God in 1972 when I was first saved. I tried so many things to make it happen, and I suffered a lot because of the mistakes I made. Others probably did too, but I've prayed for them to be healed! It took nearly 15 years for me to let God begin to work His will and His ways out in my soul.

> *You must let the truth of God dwell richly in your soul. Then and only then can God's purpose be fulfilled in your life.*

Reading the Bible over and over again is no guarantee that spiritual wisdom and understanding will become part of your life. As you begin your search of God's Word, first bind your mind to the mind of Christ and your will to the will of God. Then loose all preconceived ideas you have about God and His Word. Sometimes what we think we already know can stand in the way of the truth God is trying to show us.

> *Ask, and it will be given to you; seek, and you will find; knock, and it will be opened to you. For everyone who asks receives, and he who seeks finds, and to him who knocks it will be opened. Or what man is there among you who, if his son asks for bread, will give him a stone? Or if he asks for a fish, will he give him a serpent? If you then, being evil, know how to give good gifts to your children, how much more will your Father who is in heaven give good things to those who ask Him*
> (Matthew 7:7-11, *NKJV*).

The enemy of your soul desperately wants to confuse and discourage you about your future in Christ. He knows full well that the fears and strongholds in your life are his only tools to bring about your defeat. If you have believed and bought into a lie or you have erroneous preconceived ideas about God's plans for you, your soul will fight to protect those beliefs. Loose all of the effects and influences of the words that the enemy has spoken over you. You are a child of God (John 1:12), and you are destined to be an overcomer! Loose all wrong thinking out of your soul that would challenge that absolute truth.

> *He said to me: It is done. I am the Alpha and the Omega, the Beginning and the End. To him who is thirsty I will give to drink without cost from the spring of the water of life. He who overcomes will inherit all this, and I will be his God and he will be my son* (Revelation 21:6-7, *NIV*).

Question: *Is it possible for demons to reside in the soul if one's spirit is filled with the Holy Spirit?*

Liberty's Answer: I absolutely do not believe that demons can "reside" in the soul, the spirit, or the body of a Christian. Some do believe a Christian can be "demonized," but I cannot find any reference to this in the Bible. Many, however, insist that the New Testament is filled with references of Jesus Christ delivering Christians from demons. However, not one of them has ever given a specific Scripture to address this when I have asked them. They just repeat that "The New Testament is full of them."

These same Christians generally argue against the fact that neither Jesus nor any of the disciples or apostles ever cast demons out of a believer or held a deliverance meeting in a New Testament Church setting. When I have asked them to show me their proof that this was done, they often state that the New Testament is full of such references. I have not found them.

I do see, however, that the New Testament is full of Jesus Christ preaching the Good News. As He was going about doing this, He did deal with spirits that manifested themselves in people brought before Him. He simply spoke a command to them and they left. But not one of those recorded instances involved evil spirits manifesting themselves in a Christian believer!

What is a Christian? A Christian is one who believes and confesses that Jesus Christ is the Son of God, who died on the cross and then rose from the dead, who shed His blood to atone for his or her sins, and who purchased his or her forgiveness and salvation through His sacrifice.

> *There were no "Christians" until after Jesus Christ's death on the cross! Therefore, while Jesus was alive and ministering on earth, He could not have delivered demons out of any born-again Christian believers.*

I must assume you are asking about the souls of Christians because non-believers are not filled with the Spirit of God. Due to the many believers who have unrenewed minds, unsurrendered wills, and unhealed emotions working together to rationalize and justify not wanting to obey God's Word, I believe that a Christian's unsurrendered soul can be severely harassed by demonic spirits. The unsurrendered soul can be so riddled with open doors of access that this Christian can seem powerless to overcome the enemy's harrassment.

The concept of open doors in the soul is explained in my first book, **Shattering Your Strongholds** (specifically regarding Ephesians 4:26-27), and then further explained in **Breaking The Power**. The Christian who has multiple open doors in their soul can be demonically harassed and hammered to the point that it might seem that there were demons "within" their soul. Do not fall into the trap of believing that the manifestation of bad attitudes, wrong behavior, and wrong reactions springing out of an angry and frightened Christian soul are manifestations of demons within that soul. Casting demons out of this person will not close the doors of access, will not heal the hurts, meet the needs, or answer the questions that contribute to this person's pain and fear.

This is one area where Christians often overlook the obvious. Satan does not have only one evil spirit to send that can be bound, rebuked, or cast out. Satan has far more spirits to keep sending than any human being has time to deal with and still have any kind of life outside of the spiritual survival warfare. When Satan can get you into a spiritual survival mode, he knows that you are effectively prevented from focusing on the pursuit of your destiny with God. You've become focused on him and the ensuing battle. Satan's whole intent in harassing you is:

To keep you from focusing on your relationship with Christ and the fulfillment of your destiny in God!

To continue to war with Satan over the spirits he keeps sending to harass you is like trying to mop up an overflowing toilet without ever turning off the water that is pouring into it. The permanent answer lies in stopping the unimpeded <u>inflow</u> of what you're trying to deal with or clean up. Otherwise, you are continually mopping up the mess and never coming to a permanent solution. A permanent solution occurs when you close the doors of demonic access brought about by your own stronghold thinking (also explained in ***Shattering Your Strongholds*** and ***Breaking The Power***).

Closing doors involves using the binding and loosing principles of prayer to free yourself from this cycle. As you pray, bind your:

- ***will to the will of God,***
- ***mind to the mind of Christ,***
- ***soul to the full truth of God's Word.***

As you pray, loose (crush, smash, break into minute fragments):

- ***hindrances and devices the enemy is trying to send against you,***

13

- **wrong patterns of thinking you may have,**

- **wrong beliefs you have,**

- **the effects and influences of wrong agreements you have made with wrong teachings, and**

- **your soul's stronghold thinking patterns.**

Do this every time the enemy launches another attack against you, and you will see victory!

Question: *Do you think God has a 100% clear-cut plan for every detail of our lives? Or does He have five or six options for us to consider in different situations? You say that we always have a choice. So, how do I know if I am hearing from my soul or from God?*

Liberty's Answer: I believe God has a plan and a purpose for every detail of our lives. Just because we have a choice certainly doesn't mean we make the right choices with our own finite thinking. We think the world is full of choices for us, but as Christians, I believe our choices are really very simple:

1. **Do obey the will of God.**
2. **Don't obey the will of God.**

God's will is NOT multiple choice like we often seem to think. We come up with a list of options we think God might be willing to approve, and then we ask Him to show us whether He wants us to do "**A**," "**B**," or "**C**." I think God's answer to that question would always be: "**D—None of the above.**"

God always knows exactly what He wants done and what is best. We have two choices about how to respond to what He wants, obey or don't obey. Regardless of how spiritually right and good options may seem to us, when we choose "don't obey," not one of them will produce true spiritual fruit for the Kingdom of God.

Finite thinking has a form of understanding and can initiate what seems to be appropriate actions. Infinite or divinely inspired thinking can add the wisdom of God to our understanding to initiate His perfect plans. This addition of divine thinking and wisdom can occur only when our souls are willing and able to receive God's input. You cannot *think* a clogged soul free, you can only *obey* it free.

We are designed, as born-again Christians, to operate in both realms of thinking, but we often get bound up in the finite realm. Binding and loosing prayers provide breakthrough to our souls. This begins the process of learning to cooperate with the information God imparts through our born-again spirits. The catch here is that we must *be sure to act upon His information and follow it through to His desired purposes.*

> ***God never gives divine inspiration and supernatural intervention to pluck us out of hard situations just so we can turn and go right back down our road of self-willed wrong choices. He has very little patience for that!***

God delivers us from our follies and mistakes to set us on track with His will for future decisions. When we make those choices in alignment with His will, He accepts all of the responsibility of the consequences that come out of them. When we make self-willed choices, we become responsible for the consequences that will play out—regardless of how bad they are!

When you are in the "whale's belly" because you chose to disobey God's will, all you can do is repent and cry out for God's grace and mercy as Jonah did. Jonah 2:7-10 declares that Jonah prayed,

> *'When my life was ebbing away, I remembered you, LORD, and my prayer rose to you, to your holy temple. <u>Those who cling to worthless idols forfeit the grace that could be theirs</u>. But I, with a song of thanksgiving, will sacrifice to you. What I have vowed I will make good. Salvation comes from the LORD.' And the LORD commanded the fish, and it vomited Jonah onto dry land'*
> (*NIV*).

Can you imagine what God might have done if Jonah had picked himself up off that beach, took a quick shower, and then ran away from Nineveh again? I believe Jonah would have forfeited the grace that could have been his if he had insisted on clinging to the worthless idol of his self-will. Idolatry is deification of self.

God will receive our repentance and forgive us and give us another chance over and over. That's the good news! The bad news it that (according to the stories in the Bible) the consequences of willfully <u>repeated</u> wrong choices become tougher and tougher, harder and harder, and deeper and deeper. This is the natural outcome of God's divine plan to get your attention. It is His way to say, *"HELLO??? Don't you see that there is a cycle in your life that needs to be broken?"* Through both the hard consequences of self-willed choices and the good consequences of divinely inspired choices, God keeps trying to teach us that His choices are best.

> *If God cannot get you to cooperate with breaking that cycle through prayer, the Word, or the fellowship of other Christians, then He has no choice but to let you keep making wrong choices until the weight of the consequences drive you to seeking the truth from Him.*

One of the goals of the binding and loosing prayer principles is to disable your soul's hamster exercise wheel. This will allow you to finally be able to rest in God's will and in your faith in Him. You can rest in Him without fear when you have surrendered your will to Him, because you no longer have to figure out all the answers. Instead, you can trust Him to guide you through each question your life seems to bring. His will is already established in heaven regarding every one of them!

18

Question: *I find it hard to hear from God, to know for sure that it is Him. When I think I hear something, I always wonder if it is Satan tricking me, my soul seeking something, or God speaking to me.*

Liberty's Answer: This confusion is a smoke screen put up by your soul, with the enemy energetically contributing to it in any way he can. God has no desire to make you work your way through a maze to get to His guidance. In fact, He wants you to come out of the confusion of the smoke and mirrors of your soul and Satan. He wants you to know His voice.

This is not something to let your soul set up artificial stress over. Know this:

> *God will not punish you for wanting to be sure that it is Him speaking to you, even if it means that you misread and question some of His communion with you.*

Don't be like the car owner who is so defensive about being accused of not taking good care of her car that she wouldn't let the mechanic look under the hood. Keep binding your mind, will, and emotions to God's will, the mind of Christ, and the healing comfort of the

Holy Ghost. *Keep feeding your soul with the Word of God.* It is the part of you that needs the renewal and washing of the Word.

If you are born again, your spirit is in direct communion with God and all that His Word and will entails. Your unsurrendered soul has a choke hold on itself to keep that communion of God from permeating its "territory." Keep commanding your soul as David did to "***Bless the Lord, O my soul, with all that is within me . . .***" (Psalm 103:1).

Go to the "Breaking Soul Power" prayer on page 30 of **Breaking the Power** and pray that entire prayer once a day for at least 30 days. Your soul will begin to lose its ability to confuse you, which is a huge factor in its ability to continue controlling you. When that happens, you will pray with more understanding about closing the doors that have allowed Satan to flood your spiritual communication lines with static.

Question: *Why can't I get good Christian employees who aren't always struggling with some spiritual warfare issues in their lives? I feel more like a Father Confessor than I do a boss. What is wrong?*

Liberty's Answer: The Word says in Galatians 6:1-2 (*Amplified*):

> *If any person is overtaken in misconduct or sin of any sort, you who are spiritual—who are responsive to and controlled by the Spirit—should set him right and restore and reinstate him, without any sense of superiority and with all gentleness, keeping an attentive eye on yourself, lest you should be tempted also. Bear (endure, carry) one another's burdens and troublesome moral faults, and in this way fulfill and observe perfectly the law of Christ, the Messiah, and complete what is lacking (in your obedience to it).*

You know what? This means you are going to have to put up with some other peoples' stuff! This is something I had to learn with regard to those who work with me.

We all want perfect people to work with us so we won't be bothered by their problems. We want them to help solve our problems, that's why we hire them, right?

In the ministry, unfortunately, many say, "I have a call on my life, so I don't have time for others' stuff. I need whole, healthy, intelligent, dedicated, perfect people to work with me." Well, in this day and time, there are not many of those around whom God hasn't already assigned to help somebody else with their stuff.

To want to be completely free of any responsibility for the burdens others bear is not scriptural. Until you rethink your position, God may not send you any other workers for positions of responsibility to help you. Why? Because you have not been willing to value those He has sent. If you only want someone who is perfect and won't bug you, try another planet. God uses other people to bug us when we aren't tuned into His dealings with us.

> *We need to love people and value them just because God has entrusted them to us, instead of trying to make them over into our image of what we need.*

Don't ever say, "Why did it take you so long to do that, I could have done it in a third of the time." Do I hear an ouch? Not everyone is geared to work at your pace. This may be why God put them together with you, to slow you down a little bit. If everyone in the world ran around like they were being pursued by a rocket-fueled afterburner, we'd all go crazy. Consider these words from our Father's Book of Living a Lovely Life:

In your patience possess ye your souls
(Luke 21:19, *KJV*).

Matthew Henry explains Luke 21:19 this way: "Possess your souls, be your own men, keep up the authority and dominion of reason, and keep under the tumults of passion, that neither grief nor fear may tyrannize over you, nor turn you out of the possession and enjoyment of yourselves. **In difficult times, when we can keep possession of nothing else, then let us make that sure which may be made sure, and keep possession of our souls. It is by patience, Christian patience, that we keep possession of our own souls.** In suffering times, set patience upon the guard for the preserving of your souls; by it keep your souls composed and in a good frame, and keep out all those impressions which would ruffle you and put you out of temper."

Bind your will to the will of God and your mind to the mind of Christ, loosing all wrong patterns of thinking and beliefs you have about your own position and importance. Determine to see your employees as valuable beings entrusted to you by God for further development. Consider moments of frustration and failure to be teaching moments.

I recently took a management seminar taught by a Christian businessman, and I will never forget that he said that if our employees were failing in their sincere efforts to fulfill their duties, then we had failed in training and teaching them. That particular statement made a deep impression on me, and I vowed to work on teaching my employees how to succeed with me.

2

EVIL SPIRITS OR WRONG ATTITUDES?

Question: *Can Satan get into my mind and distort my thinking?*

Liberty's Answer: Satan wages his battle with you by means of psychological warfare. I do not think he can get into your mind and distort your thinking, but I certainly do believe that he can mess with already distorted thinking in there. If he can trick you into giving up, he has nothing to fear. If he can trick you into becoming fearful, he has psychological power over you. If he can trick you into getting angry, he can manipulate your emotions. Notice the key phrase here: *if he can trick you.*

I have lost a battle with him in this arena more than once. When I am exhausted from speaking and traveling, I particularly have to watch my temper in airports. I just keep thinking that if I make my reservations by the rules, if I pay by the rules, and if I show up and prepare to board by the rules, the airlines should play by the rules, too. Silly me! God has used airline cancellations, overbooked flights, and even a complete evacuation of thousands of people (including me!) from a terminal at O'Hare Airport in Chicago to test my ability to be cool under pressure. I've determined to learn some way to not let my blood pressure spike at these times.

One time at the Denver Airport, no picnic in the best of circumstances, all of the outgoing flights to the West Coast were cancelled. I had to be back in Sacramento the following day to start a Blitz in our LSM Training Center. I argued, cajoled, pouted, and pleaded and finally got onto a standby list—along with a stern warning that I would never get on.

As I walked away to try to find a spot to sit down, I was so aware of the stress and tension and anger level of hundreds of other people in that airport. There is some sort of reverberation or resonating that emanates out of extremely agitated souls. This "resonance" can be picked up by other souls, almost as if the negative attitude or emotion hooks into other souls and spawns a like attitude or emotion. This has to have something to do with the more intense mob mentality that grows and grows until ordinary people begin to riot and loot and destroy. It is so easy to come into wrong agreement with other angry people in this type of situation.

As I was walking, I heard a little song start in my head. Then I began to sing it out loud as I walked. *"Hail, Hail, Lion of Judah, not my will, but Thine be done! Hail, Hail, Lion of Judah, not my will, but Thine be done!"* Immediately my attitude cleared, my anger began to subside, and my energy level perked up. I learned a valuable lesson that afternoon. As I sang that song, I was breaking up my soul's attempts to marshall all of its attitudes and stronghold thinking into pushing me to get angry just like everyone else was. Thanks to the Holy Spirit's song suggestion, I side stepped my soul and Satan.

3

HEALING OF THE SOUL VERSUS DELIVERANCE

Question: *Liberty, I have been praying binding and loosing prayers for my husband for five months, ever since he left our home. He is a believer, but he has been in bondage for several years to sin. He got involved with pornography and he has lost all love and affection for anyone. He tells me he doesn't know if he can ever love anyone again. There is no one else involved that I know of, he just says that he was miserable and couldn't go on. Should I be fighting Satan for his soul?*

Liberty's Answer: Prayers unanswered are not always prayers denied, sometimes it means God is working below the surface. You are viewing your situation through your eyes of finite thinking. God's infinite thought processes have an entirely different view than you do.

Addiction begins out of attempts to deaden the pain, driving up out of a soul's unmet needs, unhealed hurts, and unresolved issues. Pornography does indeed bring a terrible numbing to the emotions, because that is what is is designed to do. It deadens the neediness and temporarily distracts from the pain and the fear of internal emptiness.

This addiction involves a wrong mind/body agreement. Whenever the mind and the body come into agreement that a certain wrong behavior is vital to the soul's sense of well being, the addiction is both psychological and physiological. This is like a double hook in the addiction. Every time the wrong behavior occurs, the brain etches a pleasure "track" deeper into itself. Your husband's problem began a long time ago, when the neediness and pain began. All he knows now is that he has a massive itch and he is convinced there is only one way to scratch it. God absolutely wants to heal him and restore him into relationship with the One who loves him most of all.

You need to be praying with the binding and loosing prayer principles, first of all for yourself. If you are not opening up your soul's defense systems and stronghold walls to divine help and healing, you may not have the strength to hold steady until God tells you what to do. One of the lies you need to loose from yourself—as many times as it takes until it doesn't return again—is that your husband's problem is your fault. Loosing prayers are like the weeding of a damaged or neglected garden. They get the weeds out.

But if you don't plant good seed in your garden once it is clear, the land just lies fallow. The weeds have nothing to stop them from coming back in. You need to be sowing for a good harvest. Sow the good seed in your own field with Scripture reading for you—with prayers for you—with affirmations of your faith in God—with time spent together with God—and with behavior that affirms that you know God has a plan for you and it is for good. Confess this: "I'm preparing for that good destiny plan. I'm getting ready to walk the good paths, to do the good works, and to live the good life."

When you get up in the morning, pray this prayer:

> *I bind my husband's will to the will of God. I bind his mind to the mind of Christ. I bind his feet to the paths he has always been ordained to walk in these days. I bind his hands to the work he's always been ordained to do in the Kingdom. I bind him to the truth of the Word with its supernatural power to heal and make whole. I loose the enemy's assignments from him, I loose all deception he has believed that he has to try to meet his own neediness and and deaden his own pain. I loose the effects and influences of word curses and wrong agreements from him. I loose all stronghold thinking from him. I loose any soul ties I have formed with him that are keeping me tied to his pain. He's yours for this day, Lord. I trust you to keep him and crowd him towards yourself. Thank you for your mercy and grace that you are extending to him. Amen.*

Then get on with your day, believing that God is working, while you're thanking Him for sustaining and comforting you and for what He is doing in your husband! Have a time in the Word with the Lord for yourself. Have a time of communion and praise and prayer with the Lord for yourself. This is not being selfish, this is being spiritually smart. If you fall apart, then you are no good to God, to your husband, or to yourself. You must stay spiritually healthy right now. You must stay very close to God.

Question: *I'm a born-again Christian. I've been saved for about six years now. I was browsing through your web site, and I have an unsurrendered soul. I cannot control my thought life.*

Liberty's Answer: Your troubling thoughts come from unmet needs and unhealed hurts, as well as from your confusion and anger over why the needs have never been met and why you were hurt in the first place. Your unsurrendered soul is afraid of what God might do if it allows Him into every area it is guarding.

As we try to cope with life, we learn (through various means) that there are certain ungodly, even destructive behaviors that can seem to temporarily take away the pain, the neediness, the pressure, the fear, etc. Unfortunately, potentially destructive, temporary relief can seem preferable to the pain and terror that comes when you fear there is no hope of relief at all. This is why some people turn to alcohol, drugs, and destructive behaviors that they know may ultimately destroy them. They learn that these behaviors dull the frightening needs and powerful drives within them at least for a short while.

Your soul creates all kinds of mental rationalizations and justifications to excuse the self-destructive actions you find yourself unable to stop. This is exactly what self-constructed strongholds are—mental rationalizations and justifications of wrong choices and wrong reactions that have been turned to so many times, they become addictive. They become things in your life that you do not know how to change. God wants to help you tear all of that down so He can come into the inner self-defense chambers of your soul and heal and deliver and free you permanently.

He will not force His way into these defenses that you have built up to try to protect yourself from further pain. You must dismantle those self-constructed defenses (strongholds) yourself. God will not destroy what your will has chosen to build. Begin by binding your mind to the mind of Christ when you pray. Loose wrong patterns of thinking and strongholds out of your soul. Pray this way for a few days, and if you feel a little stronger, then may I suggest that you get a copy of ***Breaking the Power*** and begin to pray the prayer on page 30. God will be working with you every step of the way.

4

Effective Spiritual Warfare Versus Soulish Warfare

Question: *The enemy (Satan) has been going all out for the past year to destroy our marriage, but I keep telling him this is one marriage that will stand. Is this enough?*

Liberty's Answer: Focusing on telling Satan that he cannot take your marriage down is really not as productive as you need to be. You need to keep telling **your soul** that this is one marriage that will stand, because you are praying and binding it to the will of God. Pray and also bind your spouse's soul to the will

37

of God. You need to keep declaring victory in your marriage in prayer, affirming your agreement with God on it. Don't waste your time telling the devil anything about his attempts to unravel your marriage.

> *Let him figure out what is happening by watching your new commitment to letting God's principles work for you and your spouse.*

Question: *I have read **Shattering Your Strongholds** and I am now starting on **Breaking the Power.** Are there any specific binding and loosing prayers I can pray over my marriage? I am standing in the gap for my marriage, as my spouse and I are separated (at this time), but not divorced. There is another person involved in my spouse's life, which is the second affair that I am aware of. I believe this is a result of a generational curse, because of my spouse's family history. I would appreciate anything you can tell me.*

Liberty's Answer: Your spouse's behavior is the result of his trying to meet his unmet needs that have probably been in his life for decades, years before he ever met you. Even though your spouse may want to be faithful to you, the ongoing pressure of his oldest unmet needs finally seemed too "much" to his faulty belief system of what he could handle. Rather than seeking help from you or others, your spouse has made some very wrong choices to find a means of providing his own relief.

You said that you are now starting to read *Breaking the Power* after having read *Shattering Your Strongholds*. You will find several prayers in this second book that can be used for such a situation (each one is in italics and at least a page long). You can revise any one of these prayers to pray for your spouse, for yourself, and for the other partners your spouse has been involved with.

You should also <u>loose the effects and influences of all wrong agreements off of everyone who has been a part of this circumstance</u>. This definitely applies to your spouse who has entered into wrong agreements with others to try to meet his needs. It also applies to you and your feelings of betrayal, rejection, and pain. Entering into wrong agreement with others by seeking comfort out of their support of your victim status (no matter how much they love you or want to be supportive) will not make you whole and healed. Such an attempt to garner support can actually create a form of "wrong agreement power" on which darkness feeds. This allows the work of the enemy to not only go on, but to make things worse.

> ***If you want to stop the enemy from making
> everything worse, you must not focus on how
> badly you have been betrayed and hurt.***

Extremely compassionate support can help
victimized Christians keep from self-destructing in their
initial shock of betrayal. But when that compassion and
support becomes necessary to them, they will have a
much harder time of moving toward being healed and
made whole by God.

> ***Sustained and supported agreement with a
> victim status mentality, no matter how real
> the victimization actually was, keeps the
> victim from going beyond that status.***

God needs right agreements to work through to
manifest His will on earth, particularly in this situation.
You must be the one who initially seeks to make right
agreements, while steadfastly rejecting any wrong
agreement with others. Begin to agree and speak in
prayer:

1. *That God's will be done in each and every life involved (by name if known).*

2. *That each and every mind involved would be bound to the mind of Christ.*

3. *That God's truth would be understood in each and every soul involved.*

4. *That resolution of the problem would be focused upon healing for everyone involved.*

5. *That everyone involved would repent and forgive.*

6. *That stronghold thinking would be broken in the souls of everyone involved.*

7. *That soul ties would be broken between the souls of everyone involved (even you and your spouse).*

8. *That the effects and influences of all wrong agreements made between, by, and about each and every person involved would be loosed (crushed, shattered, dissolved, etc.).*

9. *That God's grace and mercy would be poured out upon each and every person involved.*

5

TERRITORIAL WARFARE

Ephesians 3:10 (*NIV*) tells us, *"His intent was that now, through the church, the manifold wisdom of God should be made known to the rulers and authorities in the heavenly realms."* What a great verse! God's intent was and still is that the Church, the body of Christ, should rise up and through their words and actions reveal God's manifold wisdom to the rulers and authorities in high places.

Ephesians 6:12 (*KJV*) tells us, *"We wrestle not against flesh and blood, but against principalities, against powers, against the rulers of the darkness of this world, against spiritual wickedness in high places."*

Thayer tells us that the term "principalities" was used by the Apostle Paul in his writings to mean angels or demons holding dominions that were entrusted to them in the order of things.

Colossians 1:16-17 (*KJV*) tells us, *"By him [Christ] were all things created, that are in heaven, and that are in earth, visible and invisible, whether they be thrones, or dominions, or principalities, or powers: all things were created by him, and for him. And he is before all things, and by him all things consist."* Some rather nasty creatures have been allowed into places of power and will remain there until God's people present God's manifold wisdom to them. These demonic spirits have responded to the presence of multipled corporate wrong agreements of unsurrendered souls. It is up to God's people to reverse the rights of these demonic forces to set up their domains over our land.

Question: *I am an ordained minister, and right now I do not feel prepared for my call. I feel weak, defeated, alone, and **black** inside. I grew up with an addicted father who abandoned us and a mother who was anxiously trying to mend her own self, which left me to myself. I felt many unmet needs during my childhood as well as shame and humiliation. To compensate for my feelings of inferiority, I ended up* *becoming selfish, prideful, insecure, and feeling unworthy all in one basket. Then God showered me with Fatherly love and Jesus became my everything. I finally found purpose in life, as God unfolded His ministry plans for me. I finally felt like "someone" because God loved me and called me to Him.*

But now, everything seems to be slipping out of control. I feel sometimes as though I am the only one in the world with these issues. I feel there is no one to understand me. I feel bound up inside of myself. My ministry feels like it is in limbo because I am not where I should be. I feel all those old stronghold patterns of thinking again that I thought God had healed. I am just clinging to Jesus with all my might while bleeding furiously from my wounds. A prophet came to me and prophesied everything that God had said to me about my ministry. Then the prophet said I had a spirit of memory. Is this an evil spirit?

Liberty's Answer: I don't have any idea what a "spirit of memory" would be. I do know that our mind carefully catalogues and files all of our memories that our souls believe will be useful at some future time. The soul carefully builds strongholds around these memories while keeping them on artificial life support. In the tearing down of strongholds, we begin to expose the artificial life of our memories and God's blessed Holy Spirit begins to neutralize them. I once asked God for "holy amnesia," and He replied, *"No. If you had holy amnesia, how would you ever know the magnitude of what I had healed you from?"* He told me that I needed healing in my soul, not holy amnesia.

You are not the only minister to have these feelings, believe me, but you must not let this bog you down. Try to use your feelings to cause you to press harder into Him in prayer. That is where the binding and loosing prayers are so helpful, they keep tearing away at the control structure of your damaged emotions and unhealed hurts. God has a definite plan for all of our lives. The *Amplified Bible* states this is the best way in Ephesians 2:10.

> *For we are God's (own) handiwork (His workmanship), recreated in Christ Jesus, (born anew) that we may do those good works which God predestined (planned beforehand) for us, (taking paths which He prepared ahead of time) that we should walk in them— living the good life which He prearranged and made ready for us to live.*

After I finally was opening a way for God to get into the darkness of my innermost parts and heal me, I began to recognize a pattern of thinking and then discouragement and defeat would descend upon me. It always began with the words, "What's the use?" I recognized that these were words I could identify and then promptly determine that I wasn't "going there." Whenever I would hear those words in my mind, I would immediately bind my mind to the mind of Christ and loose wrong patterns of thinking.

I travel all over North America, and I am sorry to say that it took me quite awhile to become aware of the territorial oppression over the area in which I lived. Gradually I realized that an unclear backlash that I was experiencing was because I was threatening the territorial spirits constantly with this message. For several years, I would come back into the Sacramento Airport from a wonderful ministry trip, step off the plane, and immediately go into a depression. This depression would spiral downward into such thoughts as, "I think I'll just shut down the ministry and stay home and write books. I'm not making any inroads going out there, and I'm exhausted from doing it. So I'll just become a hermit writer and never leave my house." This was after great and wonderful meetings of ministry!

It was a while before I recognized that these times of depression and discouragement seemed to coincide with returning home. It was as if I had become used to oppression and the pressure while I was living under it here in Sacramento, but when I left and came back—it almost slapped me in the face as I walked back into it.

I still awake in the night from time to time, and feel the discouragement trying to settle over me, and I remember what I have recognized. And I immediately bind my mind to the mind of Christ and loose all influence of the enemy from myself and my family members. Then I go right back to sleep.

I have thought how crushing it must be for ministers and spiritual leaders who experience that same thing, but do not understand how to use the Keys of the Kingdom to deal with it. I believe that is why we see ministers giving up every day. They just don't know how to fight off the overwhelming discouragement that the enemy brings on them at every chance.

Don't give up! Recognize that you may be living in an area of great territorial oppression. If so, then God needs your ministry to succeed—you will make it with His divine help.

6

MISUSE OF MINISTRY OFFICES AND GIFTS

Question: *I was prophesied over and told to do something that I did not agree with, but the prophet said that if I did not do it, a certain unpleasant thing would come to pass. I did not do what the prophet said and the unpleasant thing did come to pass. At first I was sure that the prophecy was soulish. Now I'm not so sure.*

Liberty's Answer: There is almost always some part of any prophesying or teaching of false words or doctrine that is true. This partial truth helps to seduce people into believing, but the false parts can become very dangerous when they come to pass. Satan often manipulates people to cause false prophesies and wrong teaching to come to pass. Just remember that because something actually happens does not mean you want to take it into your soul as truth. Don't ever forget that just because a prophecy is not from God does not mean that other forces are not working to bring it to pass.

Be very cautious about those who teach doctrines that are based wholly or partly upon traditions, writings, angelic visitations, or visions that are not part of Scripture. Be particularly wary of those who caution you to realize that the Word of God was translated by men and it has some human errors in it. If you do not believe beyond a shadow of a shadow of a doubt that the Word of God is completely inerrant, then you can lose your greatest source of comfort and information when you are in real trouble.

Many are the times when I have just taken my stand on the Word of God during enormous stress and pressure, and stood there. It was the only visible and tangible thing I had to hang on to! The beauty of the Word to me is that it functions on so many different levels. I can hug and hold my Bible, I can take it to bed with me, I can read it, I can study it, I can store its contents in my mind, I can stand in faith upon the words in it, I can be led by it, and I can hear the voice of God in it. Wow!

False teachers and false prophets often quote freely from the Bible, which can be confusing. I worked in a bank as a bookkeeper when I was 20 years old. Nothing was electronic or computerized then! My great goal at the time was to become a teller. I finally was promoted to the teller line. Then I was warned that if I took a counterfeit bill, it would come out of my paycheck. My weekly salary was barely big enough to offset the taking in of a counterfeit $50 bill, so I became quite nervous. I kept asking my trainer to show me a counterfeit bill so I would know what it looked like. But she just put me on the vault window where I counted and banded everyone else's currency for hours every day, day after day. She said not to worry about the counterfeits, I would know one if I saw one.

Finally, I went on the public teller line! I was terrified, because I was so sure that I was going to be given a counterfeit. Several months later, I was given a counterfeit twenty dollar bill. I knew it immediately, because it just didn't look right. My initial training on the vault window had made me so familiar with the "real" bills that when a counterfeit bill showed up, I knew it wasn't "real."

No Christian can ever know what every false doctrine and false prophecy will look or sound like. You need to be so familiar with what <u>is right</u>, like pure biblical doctrine and the voice of God, that you will know when something is <u>not right</u>.

Why would anyone indulge in false teachings and false prophecies? Deception, denial, and unmet needs for recognition. My favorite Scripture commentator, Matthew Henry, says something about spiritual leaders (Matthew 12:24) that I find most interesting:

> *"Those who bind up their happiness in the praise and applause of men, expose themselves to a perpetual uneasiness at every favorable word spoken of any other."*

Some people, who have big gaping holes of neediness in their souls try to offset their emptiness by devaluing the worth of others through criticism and gossip. This may temporarily quiet their uneasiness and give them a false sense of some self-worth.

Question: *How do you tell the difference between discernment and being judgmental? I have the gift of discernment, though for a long time I fought* *acknowledging this gift. I didn't want the responsibility; I know I have this gift so that I can pray for people and minister to them, not so I can gossip to others about what I know. But, sometimes, I'm afraid that when I look at someone and a "knowing" rises up in me, that it is my soul's judgment rather than the Spirit's discernment.*

Liberty's Answer: First of all, there is no "gift of discernment." The spiritual gift of discerning of spirits does exist, however, and it is a very specific gift. It is not for discerning hidden things about other people such as their agendas, their motives, their truthfulness, etc. That is most often human judging done out of finite thinking processes.

This spiritual gift is a gift of discerning the source of whatever spirits are controlling or operating in a given situation. This gift is for a believer to know if a manifestation in the natural has a human soul source, an evil spirit source, an angelic source, or is from the Holy Spirit. Many Christians would adamantly say that they would know if something was from the devil or from the Holy Spirit. I would say that their souls want to believe that, but that they could be deceived and miss God's purposes and wisdom in many situations if they insist they are right.

This is why we need spiritual gifts, because our souls' finite ability to know what is going on the natural is very limited. Our souls' ability to know what is going on in the supernatural realm is almost non-existent at this time. I would suggest that you do some research on the nine spiritual gifts as found in 1 Corinthians 12, in order that you might know more about this gift God wants you to use.

The gift of discerning of spirits is very valuable when in the presence of a person purporting to be a prophet or an apostle of God. It is a gift that allows you to determine whether the Holy Spirit, a human soul, or the enemy's spirit is behind a prophetic word. Sometimes prophetic words are from the soul, human words couched in God language. Some seemingly "prophetic" words sound very spiritual, but come from a demonic source subtly trying to manipulate those who hear the words.

That which you call "a knowing" about someone can be very deceptive, and I commend you for wanting to know its source. That is the sign of a seeker of God, for some would only want to give "words" for soulish acclaim with little concern about possible deception. The binding and loosing prayers will help to define and refine your ability to identify the source of any knowing about someone. Until you gain assurance in this gift, I would suggest that whenever you feel you have this knowing, that you begin to pray that God's will would be done in that person's life, in their circumstances, in their family, in their ministry, and that they would be blessed with revelation understanding of God's love towards them and His purposes for them.

If you believe God has revealed something to you about a family member, or anyone else, pray, pray, and pray again to confirm that it really is from God. If the "word" seems to confirm something that you have been sure was going to happen to the person or that you were sure the person had done secretly, there is a strong chance that it is not from God. I'm always very suspicious of a word given from someone that lines up exactly with what I know they believe about a circumstance or a person, etc.

If you feel certain that the word was from God, consider it a prayer assignment for intercession. You should not give in to temptation to share it with others. Regardless of how spiritual we think we are, this is always a temptation to the soul which longs for recognition until it is completely surrendered to God. If God truly did give you the word as a warning for someone, you must seek His face diligently as to what He expects you to do with the warning.

> *Eagerly pursue and seek to acquire (this) love—make it your aim, your great quest; and earnestly desire and cultivate the spiritual endowments, especially that you may prophesy—that is, interpret the divine will and purpose in inspired preaching and teaching ... the one who prophesies—who interprets the divine will and purpose in inspired preaching and teaching—speaks to men for their upbuilding and constructive spiritual progress and encouragement and consolation ... he who prophesies—interpreting the divine will and purpose and teaching with inspiration—edifies and improves the church and promotes growth (in Christian wisdom, piety, holiness and happiness)*
> (Corinthians 14:1,3, 4, *Amplified*).

Question: *There is a person traveling around our area of the country, one who says(he/she) is an apostle, who is extremely critical of your message. This person has accused you of having a Jezebel spirit and says that you are teaching witchcraft by telling people to* *bind other peoples' wills to the will of God and their minds to the mind of Christ. I worry that this person's words will cause your ministry a lot of grief, perhaps even shut you down. I'm not sure just how much influence this person has internationally. What kind of spirit is involved here? How should I pray, so I do not pray wrong prayers?*

Liberty's Answer: Bless your heart for being concerned. I appreciate your wanting to pray right prayers here. First of all, since there is no spirit of Jezebel named anywhere in the Bible, this is automatically a false accusation. That means that the influences and effects of these words can be loosed.

It also seems that this person has little understanding about what witchcraft actually is. Witchcraft always tries to control and manipulate others for personal gain. There is no personal gain in binding others' wills to the will of God, their Creator. There is no personal gain in binding someone's mind to the mind of Christ. The person prayed for can always choose to turn away from being "snugged" up close and personal to God's will. This same person can always reject the mind of Christ when "snugged" up temporarily to it.

The hope we can have is that there is a brief recognition of the goodness of God's will and the peace and love of the thoughts of Christ before a frightened and desperate human soul chooses to pull away.

If my message is wrong, God will straighten me out or take me out. I am completely at peace with His ability and wisdom in doing whatever needs to be done to protect the integrity of His Word. If this other person's message about me is wrong, I pray that God will show him/her where he/she is wrong and he/she will repent before Him.

A most wise Pharisee named Gamaliel, a teacher of the Law who was honored by all people, spoke something in Acts 5 that I have never forgotton. This had to do with the treatment of Peter and the apostles who had been told to stop preaching about Jesus. Gamaliel reminded the Sanhedrin that both Theudas and Judas the Galilean, having raised up followers for their causes, were both killed and those following their causes were scattered. I especially love how Peterson's *The Message* translates Gamaliel's words in Acts 5:35-39:

Fellow Israelites, be careful what you do to these men (Peter and the *apostles). Not long ago Theudas made something of a splash, claiming to be somebody, and got about four hundred men to join him. He was killed, his followers dispersed, and nothing came of it. A little later, at the time of the census, Judas the Galilean appeared and acquired a following. He also fizzled out and the people following him were scattered to the four winds. So I am telling you: Hands off these men! Let them alone. <u>If this program or this work is merely human, it will fall apart, but if it is of God, there is nothing you can do about it</u>—and <u>you better not be found fighting against God</u>!*

So, I don't want to be fighting with this person, and I certainly don't want to be fighting with God about him/her. I just want to entrust to God both the message I believe He has revealed to me and with my attempts to deliver it as purely as I know how. If He spoke to me today to lay it all down and walk away, I would thank Him for His care and concern for me and do just that.

Thank you again for your concern and your prayers. As you pray, bind me and bind this other person to the will and purposes of God. Bind our minds to the mind of Christ. Bind us both to the truth of God's Word. Loose any half-truths, false teachings, or deceptions from each of us. Ask that God would pour out grace and mercy upon both of us. God will protect the truth of His message as He knows best. Blessing to you.

Question: *I was told that I have a spirit of fear. What is this?*

Liberty's Answer: Second Timothy 1:7 tells us that, *"God hath not given us the spirit of fear; but of power, and of love, and of a sound mind"* (*KJV*). If you would check the original Greek (I use *Thayer's Greek-English Lexicon* with *Strong's Concordance* numbering system) regarding the usage of the phrase "spirit of fear," you will find that it basically says this (*pneuma*, #4151.5):

> **To be filled with the same spirit as Christ and by the bond of that spirit to be intimately united to Christ.**

There is no room for fear in the spirit of the born-again Christian, because it is filled with the Spirit of

Christ. Fear is not a spirit, and fear does not reside in the born-again spirit of the believer.

> *Fear is a negative emotional reaction out of the soul, generally a powerful reaction to pressure upon an unresolved traumatic issue long rooted in that soul. Fear is a symptom of an internal source in the soul that needs healing.*

As long as the wrong belief, wrong understanding, or unresolved issue continues to exist, the enemy knows exactly how to pressure it today with copycat circumstances of the circumstance (from the past) that birthed it in the first place.

The internal source or root cause that has torn open a fearful individual's sense of security and courage must be <u>voluntarily exposed to God</u> before He will reach into it and heal. He will not tear down your soul's defense systems to heal you. Would it not produce more fear if an all-powerful God stomped into your soul's defense systems and blew them away to "lovingly heal you"? The binding and loosing prayer principles are very effective in dismantling these defense systems to open up the scariest hiding place.

When a Christian's soul is not fully surrendered and aligned to the truth of his or her born-again spirit, it can call up all kinds of fear-producing data from its unresolved issues. This data always seems to make sense. When this occurs, the powerful emotion of fear can quickly override the input of God's Spirit through the individual's born-again spirit.

Fear is not the opposite of faith. Faith is trust and confidence in the goodness of God towards you. While fear certainly does operate in the absence of trust and confidence in God, it is a powerful negative emotional reaction to the pain of unresolved issues out of your past. God never uses fear to prompt us to take action.

7

CURSES

Question: *I just received your book **Shattering Your Strongholds**, and I am looking forward to getting rid of a lot of ugly and negative aspects of my life. There is one question which I have asked several local pastors and have just received pat responses from them. I have also contacted a major ministry about this and they referred me to some books which I have read through, but I still have not come to any conclusion.*

What causes a curse, and does it happen when the child is still in the womb or while still at home? Can it occur after a child leaves its parents? Is there any special degree of sin involved? Does a curse go to more than one child or on to a grandchild? If a curse is placed on a child, can we assume the parent is still responsible for the parental sin, and not exonerated? I want to remove any curse from my life so that my two daughters and grandson will not be affected by my wrongdoing. I try to live according to Biblical precepts. I am 83 years old. Thank you

Liberty's Answer: Your eyes can only look up or look down. They cannot see both. So, if you are looking down at curses, you cannot be looking up at Christ at the same time. The Bible says in Philippians 4:8, *"Finally, brethren, whatsoever things are true, whatsoever things are honest, whatsoever things are just, whatsoever things are pure, whatsoever things are lovely, whatsoever things are of good report; if there be any virtue, and if there be any praise, THINK ON THESE THINGS"* (*KJV*). This is not denial of something unpleasant, this is a refocusing of your attention.

In a contemporary translation of the Bible that is called *The Message*, written by Peterson, there is a great passage where the disciples ask Jesus whose fault it was that a man was born blind. Was it the man's fault or was it his parents? Jesus replied, *"You are asking the wrong question. You are looking for someone (or some thing) to blame. There is no such cause and effect here. ASK INSTEAD what can God do now!"*

I believe you may be asking the wrong question. Consider the Word that tell us that God says, *"No weapon formed against you shall prosper, and every tongue which rises against you in judgment you shall condemn. This is the heritage of the servants of the LORD, and their righteousness is from Me, Says the LORD"* (Isaiah 54:17, *NKJV*). This Scripture can be embraced and believed to apply to our lives and the lives of our loved ones we are praying for—UNLESS we are speaking word curses, slander, and wrong agreement about others.

That sows bad seeds in the spiritual realm that will always produce a natural harvest in the one who did the sowing. *"Do not be deceived: God cannot be mocked. A man reaps what he sows. The one who sows to please his sinful nature, from that nature will reap destruction; the one who sows to please the spirit, from the Spirit will reap eternal life"* (Galatians 6:7-8, *NIV*).

If you have made mistakes and said wrong things to your children, or others have said wrong things to your children or grandchildren, you can reverse the negative power of those wrong words by right prayers. When you have sown wrong words, you need to repent, determine to turn away from doing it again, and ask our gracious God for forgiveness. Once you do this, you must then begin to concentrate on lining up all future deeds and words with the words you have prayed. Your words prayed and the ensuing deeds you do must correspond with each other to fully walk in God's truth.

We must always be watching our words while speaking of others and ourselves in a way that God would approve. Then we can pray and loose, shatter, reject, and refuse to receive the effects of any wrong words spoken about us by others—whether we know about them or not. We do not have to live under their fallout!

I bind my will to the will of God, my mind to the mind of Christ, and my emotions to the healing and balance of the Holy Spirit. I bind my body to the will of God to fulfill my destiny purposes.

I loose, crush, and smash all hindrances and devices the enemy has tried to set in my path. I loose the effects and influences of all word curses spoken about me, and I loose the effects and influences of wrong agreements spoken about me or that I have entered into.

The word "loose" in the original Greek language manuscripts means smash, crush, destroy, tear apart, dissolve, and disintegrate. After I have prayed the above, then I ask for God's mercy and grace for my life. I ask for divine direction as I read the Word and take it into my soul. And I thank God that His weapons are divinely provided to us to tear down strongholds and every high thing in our souls that would exalt itself between us and knowledge of Him (2 Corinthians 10:3-5).

I have never spent valuable research time on curses that I know I can break and tear apart through praying right prayers. I do not believe that generational bondages are generally passed on spiritually under the New Testament covenant we have, although I will not rule that out completely. I believe they are passed on through the bondage thinking patterns, bondage beliefs, and wrong attitudes passed from one generation to the next. If we are not fully surrendered to Christ in our souls, this "passing on" is inevitable with the close contact and exposure we have to our other family members' wrong patterns of thinking, speaking, and acting.

These wrong thought patterns, beliefs, and attitudes (in the unregenerated, unrenewed mind) can be loosed in prayer. As you do this, then you feed the Word into the mind to "rehabilitate" it to think on things above. To focus on Jesus Christ and His plans and purposes for your life. In prayer when you loose something out of your soul, replace it with the reading of the Word and right actions. This keeps that ugliness from growing back just like stubborn weeds do.

Question: *My family has always had a spirit of criticism. Everyone has spoken word curses to each other. How can I get rid of this spirit?*

Liberty's Answer: Here is a great story. Four men were climbing a very high and snowy mountain, and two of them fell into a deep chasm in the snow. The other men gathered around the opening and discussed how hopeless the situation was. The men in the chasm would surely freeze to death before anyone could return to the bottom of the mountain and get help. They told the two men that they were as good as dead, and they should just thank God for their lives, lie down, and go to sleep. The two men ignored the comments and tried to climb up out of the chasm with all of their might. The other men kept telling them to give up, that they were as good as dead.

Finally, one of the men took heed to what the men were saying and gave up. He laid down, closed his eyes, and died. The remaining man continued to struggle as hard as he could to climb up the side of the crevasse. Once again, the men desperately yelled at him to stop the pain and just die. That seemed to make the man struggle even harder. He finally made it up to the top and climbed out.

The two men said, *"Didn't you hear us? Why didn't you just give up like George? Why did you keep trying so hard to get out?"* The man explained to them that he was very hard of hearing. He had thought they were shouting encouragement at him the entire time. He said that he believed if they thought he could do it, then he probably could.

There truly is the power of life and death in the tongue. An encouraging word to someone who is down can lift them up and help them make it through the day. On the other hand, a destructive word to someone who is down can be the straw that breaks their will to go on.

> *"The tongue has the power of life and death . . . "*
> (Proverbs 18:21).

Be careful of what you say. Speak life to those who cross your path. If you happen to run into someone who is down in a crevasse of discouragement or despair, toss him a lifeline of hope and encouragement. If you are hearing a lot of discouraging words, then you become "hard of hearing" and keep climbing upwards. The next effort you make may get you out of that deep hole. We should all be "hard of hearing" when words being spoken are negative.

There is no spirit of criticism to be found in the Bible. But there are wrong patterns of negative thinking in human souls that breed words of criticism. In prayer, loose (dissolve, crush, shatter, etc.) the hold your soul has on these wrong patterns of thinking. Don't worry about why you think that way, just loose your soul's hold on these thought patterns. This creates space in your soul, which you should immediately begin to fill (this is called "occupying the territory") with an action of right speaking on your part. Begin to speak words of encouragement and affirmation to your family members. Begin to speak simple, sincere compliments to your family members. Ignore any suspicious retorts they might speak back to you. If they do, just get to a place of prayer as soon as you can to begin binding their minds and emotions to the mind of Christ, binding their wills to the will of God—and then loosing wrong patterns of thinking from their souls.

We should all be silent when negative words crowd up in our throats. I always think of Bambi's little friend, Thumper the rabbit, in the original Bambi movie (which came out when I was a child). Thumper used to say, "If you can't say somethin' nice, don't say nuthin' at all!" Well spoken, Thumper.

Question: *I have been told that I have a curse on my life. I believe it is several generational curses. I am a firm believer in God and Jesus Christ, and I am in prayer every day, yet I am poor, sick, and fearful. I have done some background research on my family history and I have found that my great-grandfather was a slave trader. How do I break these generational bondages?*

Liberty's Answer: You have come into a wrong agreement with someone regarding the idea that you have a curse on your life. This allows another person as well as evil spirits to manipulate your beliefs and ideas. Proverbs 26:2 declares, *"Like a flitting sparrow, like a flying swallow, a curse without cause shall not alight"* (*NKJV*). If you are a born-again, washed in Christ's blood, Christian, you have been forgiven for past sins, even the sins of your father and grandfathers.

Generational bondage is usually generational wrong thinking patterns, such as wrong attitudes acquired from repeated family exposure. I do not believe they can be transferred like curses upon a Christian

71

unless the Christian gives them a place to land by coming into agreement with the possibility.

You state that you are "poor, sick, and fearful" even though you are a firm believer. Those really are not the words of a firm believer. It's easy to get caught in the victim trap and think that you are suffering because of what others have or have not done. God did not create you to be a victim! He created you to be an overcomer:

> *"Then God said, Let Us make man in Our image, according to Our likeness; <u>let them have dominion</u> over the fish of the sea, over the birds of the air, and over the cattle, over all the earth and over every creeping thing that creeps on the earth. So God created man in His own image; in the image of God He created him; male and female He created them. Then God blessed them, and God said to them, <u>Be fruitful and multiply; fill the earth and subdue it; have dominion over the fish of the sea, over the birds of the air, and over every living thing that moves on the earth"</u>*
> (Genesis 1:26-28, *NKJV*).

To have dominion means you are not a victim, you are a person to whom God has given power over the earth to subdue it. Wrong agreements open doors in your soul for strongholds to be built that are protecting beliefs of defeat, unworthiness, and weakness. You must stand up and declare who you are without fear and without the baggage of the past sins of your forefathers.

Your soul is complex but not impossible to handle. God has given you dominion, and that includes the right to choose to surrender your soul to Him. The power of the Holy Spirit that courses through you is strong enough to raise Jesus from the dead (Romans 8:11). This same Spirit is also strong enough to handle what is happening inside you.

Bind your mind to the mind of Christ and bind your will to the will of God. Bind yourself to the fact that you are a new creature in Christ, unfettered by the sins of a bygone era. Loose the effects of wrong agreements in your soul, and loose the power the enemy has exerted over you because of those wrong agreements. Loose the deception and wrong thinking that has been a part of your soul and get free from wrong mindsets. God did not create you out of weakness; He created you out of His power. In the same way, Jesus did not die for you out of weakness; He died for you out of His power to overcome death. You have the power to live a full and fruitful life. Apprehend it and live like you know it is yours!

Question: *How do you bind a witch from doing harm to other people?*

Liberty's Answer: Jesus said that whatsoever I would bind and loose on earth would be bound and loosed in heaven (Matthew 16:19). This is authority to bind and loose on earth what has already been bound and loosed according to God's will in heaven. Therefore, I would bind the witch's:

- **will to the will and purposes of the one and only Almighty God and Creator of the universe,**

- **mind to the mind of Jesus Christ,**

- **hands to the work God has ordained for her to do in these end times,**

- **feet to the paths God has ordained for her to walk, and**

- **her whole being to the truth of God's sovereignty, Christ's divinity, and the inerrancy of the written Word of Scripture.**

I would loose from the witch's soul:

- **the effects and influences of wrong thought patterns,**
- **wrong attitudes,**
- **wrong beliefs,**
- **wrong teachings,**
- **the effects and influences of denial, deception, and half-truths,**
- **the effects and influences of wrong agreements, word curses, and soul ties.**

Most, if not all, of the works of demonic manifestations and demonstrations are worked through the souls of humans. Witches are human beings who have agreed to surrender their souls' power to Satan's works of darkness. I would use the Keys of the Kingdom (the rule of God) to disrupt the bondage of their darkness and shed some light into their souls.

8

Generational Bondage Thinking

Question: *I suffered so much emotional and mental abuse from my parents when I was little. Isn't there anything that can be done spiritually to stop people from doing this to their children? What is wrong here? Why doesn't God stop it?*

Liberty: It is tragic that there are children who are being damaged by <u>adults who are damaged themselves</u>. It is the worst kind of generational bondage that most people who abuse have been abused themselves by others who were abused. This becomes an issue of **who will stop the cycle now** more than it is an issue of who has not stopped it in the past.

Both the blame for and the answer to this issue rests directly on the body of Christ. God gave us a very clear solution to our nation's many sins and abusive behaviors in 2 Chronicles 7:14 (KJV):

> *"If my people, which are called by my name, shall humble themselves, and pray, and seek my face, and turn from their wicked ways; then will I hear from heaven, and will forgive their sin, and will heal their land."*

When the body of Christ finally become serious about understanding and obeying this Scripture, the ongoing cycle of the hurtful actions of damaged people will be broken.

When you and I obey this Scripture in faith and confidence in the faithfulness and mercy of God, I believe some child or perhaps several children are divinely protected from harm somewhere in the world. This is not just a nice sounding passage of Scripture, this is a God-promise filled with divine power to heal and protect when anyone—anywhere—obeys it. Few people are praying and fulfilling their part of this passage, and little healing is going forth. But I am convinced that healing does go forth in our land every time a believer accomplishes the conditions God has asked of us here. God says that His Word never returns unto Him void, but it always accomplishes the purpose for which He sent it.

It is not God's will that little children should ever suffer, but when His people do not consistently stand in the gap for the small babies and the young children and the teenagers, the negative consequences of other peoples' sins begins to splash into their lives almost like acid. We all need to repent of our lack of faithfulness in repenting and turning from our own wicked ways, to seek His face and pray in a consistent manner, so that He will heal our land.

> *"Or are you so blind as to trifle with and presume upon and despise and underestimate the wealth of His kindness and forbearance and long-enduring patience? Are you unmindful or actually ignorant of the fact that God's kindness is intended to lead you to repent—to change your mind and inner man to accept God's will?"*
>
> (Romans 2:4, *Amplified*).

9

FINAL THOUGHTS

Here is a testimony that has been an encouragement to me and my ministry team:

Thank you so much for studying God's Word and rightly dividing the Word of Truth! I have been a Pentecostal Christian for twenty years, and I've read so many books on spiritual warfare and prayer. But I finally came to what I felt was the end of my spiritual rope as a Christian. Day to day life was so hard. Being optimistic and focusing on the good things for a year didn't seem to change anything, because negativity took over as reality kept slapping my face!

*I finally gave up railing against my circumstances and just stood and waited for His deliverance. I did get some breathing space from God. And then my husband picked up your book **Shattering Your Strongholds** in a stack of great Christian books for giving away!*

As soon as I started reading that first day and praying the prayers, the Holy Spirit's sweet presence touched me for the next two hours confirming the Word. I read and prayed through the book again, using a highlighter the second time around. Like another one of your questioners on your web site, I felt irritable and snappish when the first strongholds were being shattered. I have since then dealt with three other painful memories as God is continuing His work.

*I ordered **Breaking the Power** and am praying my way through both books daily. I have seen many wonderful answers to prayer. A family member had been falsely accused of a crime, and the police were involved. I had sent your first and second books to this family member, and they arrived that week. We began to pray the binding and loosing prayers together about this nightmare, and yesterday the police notified this family member and said that they had found the accusations to be unfounded. Praise God! I've ordered your third book and am looking forward to more!*

LIFE-CHANGING BREAKTHROUGH SERIES

KEYS OF THE KINGDOM TRILOGY

". . . a refreshing look at a truth that may be just what you need to walk in freedom . . ."

IVERNA TOMPKINS

SHATTERING YOUR STRONGHOLDS

Freedom From Your Struggles

Liberty Savard

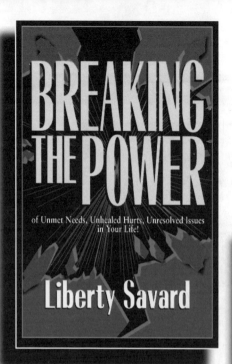

Liberty Savard

BREAKING THE POWER
of Unmet Needs, Unhealed Hurts, Unresolved Issues in Your Life!

Liberty Savard

You've shattered and broken your strongholds
Now, it's time to begin
PRODUCING THE PROMISE

Liberty Savard